I0504956

Managing Your Brand !

You can Pimp me,

But you must pay me.

By

Reginald Grant, MSEd

Editor: Miriam Glover,

Miriam Glover Marketing

Cover Photo: Bruce Stephens,

Cherished Memories Plus

Grant, Reginald L.

Managing Your Brand. You can Pimp me, But you must pay me.

Reginald L. Grant © 2019.   pp. 44

ISBN 9781693234897

1. Education   2. Branding 3. Success

_____

Table of Contents

Leveraging Your Network

Reginald Grant

Introduction

Most of us do not consider ourselves a "Brand", but the reality is you are a "Brand." When you go for job interviews what are you selling? You, right! When you start a new company and need investment or a loan from the bank what are you selling? The idea, and the management team; in short, "You." As a leader, how you choose to manage your personal brand will influence your daily leadership decisions and career management plans. Nike, Apple, Michael Jordan, KISS are all brands, so are you. Do you think they manage their public image? Do you think the management of that image has anything to do with generating revenues?

Are you taking advantage of all of your opportunities by managing your "Brand?" If you are not managing your "Brand" who is? Can you leverage your "Brand" to take advantage of opportunities? Do you use the internet? Social Media? What's online about you? Not being mindful on how you manage your personal "Brand" can have negative consequences such as loss of focus, loss of impact and loss of career or business momentum.

Let's explore how can you proactively manage your brand?

Leveraging Your Network !
By Reginald Grant

| Phase 1 | How do you benefit from Your Network |

| Phase 2 | Your "Brand" has value |

| Phase 3 | Identify the Opportunities that are Right For You |

| Phase 4 | Leveraging Opportunities |

Why YOU need to set goals!

Goal setting is powerful. It is the way to motivate yourself, keep yourself on track and clearly identify what you want your future to look like. Setting goals makes it real and writing it down helps to clarify where you are going.

Understand that goals will change and are not to be set in concreate like an immovable object but are a set of milestones. The old adage rings so very true, "Plan to succeed or don't plan and plan to fail."

If you are in business, you need to clarify those goals by developing a business plan. All a business plan does is identify short term objectives and goals and long-term goals for the business. So, whether you are seeking investment dollars or outside financing, you need to write a business plan.

How do you benefit from Your Network

Turn relationships into business opportunities

Are you connecting the circles ?

Friends

Friends

Those that want to be in your network.

Associates

Associates

Those that want to be in your network

My Brand

Many years ago, I was being interviewed by a reporter, after I signed as a free agent with the Miami Dolphins, and he said to me "I have never met anyone who promoted themselves so well." I took it all in stride and it was not until many years later that the light went off and I started thinking of myself as a "Brand." I was selling myself all along but, I did not think of myself clearly as a "Brand." I was just trying to highlight my best qualities when appropriate.

There are thousands, if not hundreds of thousands of people named Reginald Grant or Reggie Grant in the United States. But I own that name, if you search online with either version of the name, I own the space. I will come up first and more often than anyone else. I've owned rgrant.com for nearly two decades and purchased the domain reginaldgrant.com as soon as I could get the name.

Two years ago, I decided that I was going to go in a different direction. I created goals for where I wanted to be and a step by step plan outlining how to get there. The goals and strategies had to be adjusted along the way, but ultimately my goals were achieved. I carved out and positioned myself to serve the needs of specific clients and positioned myself as an expert in specific areas. I created a clear brand identity and was able to devise a clear and sync story.

Identify the Opportunities that are Right For You.
How do you leverage your network to benefit you financially?

Identify opportunities

Analysis of the opportunity

Develop a plan

Execute the plan

Building a Brand

How do you Build a "Brand?" These Few Questions May Help you clarify your steps.

What do you want to be identified as?

What are you or your company all about? What are you goals and how do you want to be perceived? When, where, and how can people get your product and or services. Do you clearly articulate your "Brand" story?

Who are you serving and why?

Have you identified a specific target market and or people you will serve? Can you identify a clear segment or segments that want or need your product or services? Is the target focused enough that it is actionable?

What service or product are you selling?

You have to clearly identify what you are delivering. What is your product and how will you deliver it? Have you set realistic goals and figured out as many of the steps required to deliver it to your clients?

Three Steps
The path to cash.

Your Network   Converting to Business   Revenues

Leveraging Social Media

Marketing experts will generally define a brand as a company or individual image. But a brand is so much more than just your company image. It also includes your customers experience and the expectations you set when doing business with you or your company. It is a promise.

Social media is the culmination of multiple forms of traditional media that is available everywhere and immediately. Video, Print, television, radio have all converged to create Social Media. It is instant access and can have instant impact – both positively and negatively.

A well throughout social media strategy is a requirement for long term success in most industries in today's business world. So, you must decide where to focus and which social media platforms to use. LinkedIn, Twitter, Facebook, Instagram, WhatsApp, Snap Chat all have advantages and weak points. The demographics, and popularly of specific social media platforms is always evolving. Think about your objectives, do the research and plan. Always remembering that goals should not be set in stone, be flexible and willing to try different things.

Convert your Contacts into CASH !

You can make dollars because of who you are and who wants to be associated with you !

Where can you find leads?

Your network – People you already know
Golf Tournaments
Business Networking Events
Parties
Social Events
Etc......

SOCIAL MEDIA PLATFORMS

Turning Your Brand into Revenues

Are you placing the right value on your time energy and expertise? Unclear: **"Do they have Skin in the Game?"**

The first question I always ask myself when talking with people that approach me with a new project is, "Do they have Skin in the Game?" Have they invested their own money into the project?

If the answer is no, then a big "RED FLAG" is thrown in the game. I question why do they call themselves an Entrepreneur?   My perspective on business is simple. If money does not change hands, there is no business relationship. Let me clarify. If you have ever seen Shark Tank you have seen how the investors (Sharks), make decisions and how many of the presenters are not prepared to make decisions that will serve their best interest.

Too often they make decisions based on incorrect assumptions, a lack of understand how real business works, and inflexibility. They too often don't understand the correct value of the right strategic mentor, partners, and expertise. They too often come into the Shark Tank with "No Skin in The Game", i.e. their own monies invested in the concept, or idea. Yet, they fully expect someone that they do not even know to back that idea. Doesn't that seem unrealistic in the real world, even a tad arrogant?

This is how I see the Tank, it is not about the money.

1. The Sharks have knowledge and expertise

2. The Sharks brands have significant value

3. The Sharks have an expensive network and understanding how to leverage that network.

4. The Sharks have the ability to make phone calls and access people, companies and industries at will.

5. The Sharks rightfully value their time.

6. The Sharks Tank provides "exposure to millions" of people that the presenters would never have the opportunity to be exposed to, over and over (reruns).

I do not equate myself to them because I do not have that level of financial resources, but I do look at myself in the following terms.

1. My most valuable asset is my TIME.

Then:

2. My expertise and knowledge.

3. My relationships and access to people

4. Access to my time, expertise and network is valuable and costs.

Why do people expect others to give away their assets, relationships or knowledge? It costs - cash, and/or equity – the compensation must be valuable enough for someone to commit time and energy to a project. Are you placing the right value on your time energy and expertise? Too often people get swept-up with the hype and possibilities of a project. Learning to place a real value on your assets is so very important in business. I often get approached by those looking for a handout instead of a handup or those not willing to pay for the expertise they need.

Networking vs Relationship Development

You have to be in the Room!

Simple yet profound when you think about it. "You Have to be In the Room." So very much about successful business is relationships. People often say that I am an expert networker, they are wrong I am all about building relationships. Networking at its core is about meeting a lot of people and distributing information, emails, phone numbers, and cards. Well, for me it's the next step, actually building, lasting relationships. Truly connecting with people, finding out if you are of like minds and core values. If you have synergy and can develop a lasting relationship, you will not always be in agreement but, having a real relationship where problems can be resolved. The one constant about being in business is that there will be obstacles and problems to be resolved, do you have the resiliency, determination and focus to work through the challenges. Without a real relationship, the issues become much more difficult to resolve and are far too often the primary reason business fail.

At the #AIShowBiz Summit 2018, event in Hollywood in 2018, I was in the room and pitched for SIDOG, a gaming tech company. One of the speakers, Xavier Kochhar, founder, The Video Genome Project (Hulu) AI, stated it during his presentation, "You Have to be In the Room." I tracked him down after his presentation and asked him for more details and he reinforced it. Being in the room whether you are the speaker, or a worker allows you human interaction and the opportunity to begin to establish a relationship. You want to learn, to grow and do business with people then you have to be in the room. We are too often confused about technology and its ability to replace humans; nothing is more powerful than a direct one-on-one conversation for relationship building. So, if you want to grow your business, "Be In the Room." For me, that meant increasing my visibility and I committed to traveling to ten cities last year. Now, my business is growing as a direct result. The stress and disruption to routines is difficult, at best, but everything has a cost. Are you willing to pay the cost?

That week I flew 6,000 miles round trip LA to the east coast and rode on a train just so I could "be in the room". The rewards were amazing on many fronts. I had the opportunity to meet with the Willard Bailey, President of Central International College and his Director of Fund Development Andre Moore in Richmond, Virginia. After months of online meetings, calls, and emails, we finally were able to take our relationship to the next level because we were all in the room.

I then had the opportunity to attend the 28th Annual Watkins Award for Scholar Athletes weekend in Washington, D.C. The reinforcement of existing relationships and development of new relationships was exciting and fruitful. On Friday, my company held its eSi Pitch event and I had the opportunity to interact and learn from some dynamic people. Panelist Paul Ruffin, ECI Networks from Minnesota, Attorney Chad Jones, from Mississippi, (and his lovely wife Ashley Jones from Swamp People), Gary Lewis McPherson II financial advisor from Maryland, John Matthews CEO CEO/President, Prothymos Technologies and his partner Chris Lee, from Pennsylvania, David Segal and his fiancé Lauren from York, PA, Yori Adegunwa CEO, Iroy Running and others. It was a dynamic group and offered, yet again, another chance to develop relationships.

Saturday was another opportunity to meet with people, Leon, and Angie McQuay, head of the Leon McQuay Foundation from Tampa, FL, Cedric Watkins, author of the new book out next month, "A Legacy of Giving", about the life of Franklin D. Watkins, Derrick E. Frost, former NFL player? & financial advisor. Watkins Award alumni Josh Dobbs (Steelers), Devier Posey (CFL, Gray Cup MVP 2018). Zack Banner (Steelers), James Vaughters (Calgary, CFL), and many others. The evening allowed me to re-establish relationships and connect with new contacts. I had the privilege to reconnect with Watkins Alumni Marcus Houston, now the father of three and a practicing attorney, Luke Powell a college athletic administrator in the mist of changing positions, Savon Huggings, CEO of #DOWIT and now a Watkins Board member, James Vaughters who is continuing his professional football career in the CFL he recently joined the Board of Directors of the NAAAA. The young guns, Watkins Award current college student-athletes RaKavius Chambers, Mataeo Durant, and Brandon Hill at Duke, Quincy Patterson II, Virginia Tech, and Messiah deWeaver, Old Dominion. Wow, so proud of all of our Alumni and their accomplishments.

Being in the room makes all the difference. Are you placing yourself in the room to drive relationship development and grow your business?

Does Your Brand Reflect Success?

Creating a Culture of Success, Around You.

Most of us strive to be successful in whatever we endeavor to attempt. Creating a culture of success in our homes, our work environments' or teams is a difficult task at best. As parents, we want to help our kids to thrive and succeed in everything. As a teacher in the classroom, I wanted to create an environment that allowed every student to achieve individual success. To help them grow and improve on a daily basis. As a business professional or leader, we want the environment to lead to profits build on the success of the group. As a coach, we need to win to be considered successful, winning is built on the individual efforts of many for a common goal.

Thus, success is measured in many ways and for many purposes. For parents, it's the light going off in your children's eyes when they make a new discovery or achieve a small milestone, from taking their first step, doing well on an exam, scoring the winning goal or in a thousand other ways. I see creating a successful mindset for ourselves and our children as part of our reasonability as parents. There isn't a manual for parenting, despite all of the books and modern tools, it is still a trial and error process. Children respond to things differently and are as individual as our fingerprints, so we must adapt, adjust and strive to figure it out. Creating a home culture is an ever-evolving process and we must place our children in situations they can safely learn and grow in. Despite our culture of instant gratification where everyone wins all of the time, failure is to a part of that process. Successful people embrace failure as one of the steps to success. We must nurture our children and yet help them understand that success is a process.

I read an interesting article on Clemson football Coach Dabo Sweeney and the adversity he faced as a child and young man. The article was published before they won the national championship. The ever-present theme of the story was perseverance and his determination to make the best of every opportunity. Thus, he has turned a floundering program into a national powerhouse by developing a success-oriented culture. By nurturing and caring for the people he's charged to oversee and motivate, from his players to his staff. The same qualities are often displayed by the contributing authors of my book *Success Stories Insights by African American Males.*

When I was a high school head football coach my biggest challenges were all of the outside influences and the historic culture of the programs I was charged to change. So many of the elements of the historic culture of the programs were hidden and lay below the surface. I was too focused on the internal elements, and it was if I was a bad politician and did not address the impact of outside influences well enough. Sweeney has done that and created a culture of success.

The same problems inherent in development of a sports team permeate a business. It's a group of individuals with very diverse backgrounds that need to work together for a common goal, business success equals profits. Creating a culture of success for a business is a daunting task and leadership must provide the direction that leads to success. Creating that culture takes a focused vision that must be dynamic and purposeful.

In our schools I have often seen leadership that was focused on achieving goals related to success on the standardized test. Yet, they too often forgot that individual success is the determining factor in the success of the group. Much is made about creating a culture of success without including opportunities to adequately motivate the individual students. Many times, they used artificial rewards and arbitrary collective goals. Too often they did not connect the students to alumni who had gone through the same situations and circumstances to succeed. A clear picture was not painted and vision of the world of opportunities' open to the students may not have even been explored. Successful schools, especially in urban and challenging environments, must be more diligent in connecting the students to real world success stories and people.

Different societies, nations and even the subcategories' within in those groups see success so very differently. Even within groups of people of similar backgrounds, religions, socioeconomic status and ethnic group's success can be viewed with different lenses. How do you define success? Is it money, fame fortune, a relationship with God, who knows but you? But one thing I do know is that success does not happen without commitment, a commitment to your family, business, mission, or team and it always includes a vision and a goal. Does your vision of success help others? Or are you looking for success in all the wrong places and things?

We need to create the same types of cultures of success in our business circles. I was a businessman for many years prior to entering education. As I looked back in reflection, I realized that when I was most successful, I was surrounded by other liked minded people. I was fortunate enough to have been surrounded by people who wanted to make money, but not at any cost. They had a great work ethic, morals and cared about others. It all boiled down to one common thread, people. It was about relationships and a culture of success.

As a result of my past experiences I joined forces with a core group to develop a platform for business success. The Business Circle a private, invitation-based business networking group out of Los Angeles. We currently have members in about 10 states and

France. Our goal is not to be huge, but to foster win-win business relations where the drive for profits does not blind us. I also became more involved with the only former professional organization that works directly with owners of a professional league,the Retired NFL Players Congress. Which, in partnership with the largest manufacture of designer licensed jackets outside of China, JH Design has a direct license with NFL Properties. (playerscongress.com)

I firmly believe that one can have success and have a positive impact on society without impending others. Are you creating win-win scenarios for success?

Leveraging Your Network !
By Reginald Grant

Phase 1	How do you benefit from Your Network
Phase 2	Your "Brand" has value
Phase 3	Identify the Opportunities that are Right For You
Phase 4	Leveraging Opportunities

Growth! I Read a Great Business Book
recently, *"What Matters in Business."*

Are you looking to grow as a leader? Do you seek out opportunities to develop and become better at working with and managing people? The mentors I had the privilege to work with always stressed the requirement to continue to develop as a critical step in the journey for success. As a classroom teacher I learned from my students, and as a business leader I always tried to surround myself with great people. We must actively seek out knowledge, I am often surprised where I find inspiration.

Bob Burg and John David Mann do an exceptional job of using a creative story to highlight *What Matters in Business*. I could not put the book down; the book is only about 120 pages, but the point of *It's Not About You, it's all about your customer* was in laser focus. Every businessperson and anyone looking to improve the trajectory for success needs to read this book. I do not know Mr. Burg or Mr. Mann personally, so this is a totally unsolicited testimonial. The way they framed the short story and illustrated how important it is to take oneself interest out of the picture leads to engagement and empowerment of others that elevates you.

The old adage about "you get back what you give tenfold" rings so very true and the way they articulated that point is admirable. I was so engaged by the presentation I literally did not put the book down until I finished. I had a million things on my plate, and I put every one of them were put on hold, that is how valuable the message was to me. I was immediately pulled into the story and it kept my attention from start to finish. There are numerous life lessons illustrated in the story and most I have seen a hundred or thousand times but the way they crafted this story made all of the difference. I had many 'a-haw' moments as I read along, with each one reinforcing one of my core values of "being of service to others matters." Acts of selflessness are so often rewarded in ways we could never plan.

Check out the book, a quick read but oh, so powerful.

An Open Letter to Athletes,

You can Pimp me, but you must pay me.

I still have a negative connotation in my mind with the word Pimp. Although, the younger generation often uses the term as empowering and thinks of it in a positive light. I still have visions of abuse and using a human being in negative ways when the term comes to mind. But, in this instance, I use the term because I feel "if I'm going to get used, I must get compensated fairly for it. "

As professional athletes and former professional athletes, we are often approached by ruthless, unscrupulous and untrustworthy individuals and companies. That want to use us to further their own agendas without compensating us for our time, energy, name (Brand) and network. And, sometimes there are well meaning people who place no value on our time and act as if we owe them something.

Fact is anyone including us who has achieved anything usually worked hard and with tremendous sacrifice to achieve our goals. As Vince Lombardy is quoted as saying, "the only place success comes before work is in the dictionary." That statement is so true. Each of us has worked hard to achieve our accomplishments on and off the field. We deserve to be rewarded for our success, it's the 'American Way'.

I was an English teacher, and author for over seventeen years. A few summers ago, I was teaching a group of young people from Paris and one member said to me, "You have lived the American Dream." It was eye opening. I had never thought of my live in such terms, but he was right. Here I am, a poor kid from Greenbrier projects in Atlanta, then from the High Point Projects in Seattle yet I've lived a great life. Graduated from the University of Oregon, played professional football (NFL, CFL) and visited every major city in America. I've even had the opportunity to visit some international cities too. I've worked in corporate America and owned numerous businesses.

Wow! Each former or current collegiate and professional athlete has a story like this; it has not always been easy and far from perfect, but we did it. Is it fair for someone else to benefit and not compensate us? No!

I thank each and every one, including my parents who sacrificed to give me these opportunities. America is all about competition, rewarding those who dare to be different, and bold enough to follow a dream. As a marketing professional, I clearly understand the value of my knowledge, expertise, and Brand. A few years ago, I had the opportunity to reconnect with pro football legend and Hall of Famer Kellen Winslow at the Pro Athletes Business Group's conference in Oakland. He made a profound statement during his keynote speech about how many of us under- value ourselves and end up selling ourselves short. Allowing others to profit and benefit from our efforts, without receiving compensation. The light went off for me.

In the past several months, I have been approached by a dozen businesses or individuals who fit that category. An athletic training program, a high-tech sports product company, a pro-development league, a golf related project, an athletic manufacturing company, and a music program for youth to name a few that wanted to leverage me, my contacts and brand for their own benefit. They wanted to compensate me very little, on the back end or under their terms. They wanted me to drive their dream yet did not want to invest in their own dream by fairly compensating me. I must note, there were some good projects too, but most did not fit me. But those people that wanted to use me far outnumbered the people who were willing to treat me, as I have learned to demand to be treated.

I say to each of you, do not let these users win. You deserve to be paid, you earned it. Leverage your network to your benefit. It's ok to say no and get what you have coming to you. I wish you the very best and encourage you to find that project or deal that allows you to leverage your hard work for your benefit. Look for that win-win situation.

It doesn't matter where you come from it only matters where you go.

Reginald Grant, MS Ed.

SIX (6) Athletes that Get It.

Josh Dobbs– Currently QB in the NFL. Josh clearly understands relationship development and content creation. I saw this firsthand earlier this year at the VIP Reception for the 28th Annual Watkins Award weekend. There was a dozen or so business professionals I had invited to the event. Josh interacted with many people that night, and within 24 hours Josh had texted, emailed or reached out to the new contacts. He clearly understands relationship development and "Brand" building. https://twitter.com/josh_dobbs1?lang=en

Marv Fleming - Marvin was the first NFL player to play in five Super Bowls, and won four; two with the Green Bay Packers and two with the Miami Dolphins. He was also a member of the 1972 undefeated team. Marv is a highly sought-after speaker and Director of the Signature Jacket Program for the retired NFL Players Congress. http://marvfleming.com , playerscongress.com

Marques Ogden was an American football offensive lineman. He played with the Jacksonville Jaguars, the Baltimore Ravens, the Buffalo Bills, and the Tennessee Titans. He is the brother of Hall of Fame offensive tackle Jonathan Ogden. A graduate of Howard University, he has excelled in business after football and often speaks nationally. https://marquesogden.com/

DeVier Stewart Posey is an American football wide receiver who is currently a member of the Montreal Alouettes of the Canadian Football League. He was drafted by the Houston Texans in the third round of the 2012 NFL Draft. He played college football at Ohio State. His Pocket Full of Poseys Foundation is making an impact on kids and families.
https://www.pocketfullofposeys.org/

Ronald Jones II is an American football running back for the Tampa Bay Buccaneers of the National Football League. He played college football at USC. Ronald is launching his own merchandise line and positioning himself for success after professional football.
https://www.rojo27.com/

Thomas Williams is the author of *Permission to DREAM* and *The Relentless Pursuit of Greatness*, Professional Speaker, NFL Player Engagement Ambassador, and Philanthropist. Thomas is a former National Champion (USC) and former NFL player that set goals and worked relentlessly to achieve them.
http://thomasrwilliams.com

Understanding Intellectual Property "IP"

Intellectual Property – Changing the way the world does business!

Excerpt from *Youth Entrepreneurial Impact Program*, textbook by Reginald Grant, MS Ed.

For previous generations manufacturing was the driving force in economic success, that all changed. Today in America and the world the driving force behind economic success is directly tied to the development of IP or intellectual property. Creating economic value from things developed is crucial in these times.

Previously, the main sources of competitive advantage were the availability of natural resources and a skilled labor market. While these factors remain important, intellectual property must now be included as a critical driver of business profitability. For firms, intellectual property contributes to distinct products. For the economy, intellectual property fosters innovation and risk-seeking behavior, and entrepreneurs and investors must choose wisely. One of the inherent advantages of intellectual property businesses is the low initial startup capital required. Of course, once a certain level is reached, significant traditional financial investment is required. For many companies, it is also a factor that leads to significant challenges of strategy, finance, and business organizations.

"The global economy has shifted from the manufacturing-based economy of the last century to the knowledge-based, innovation driven economy of the 21st century. Whereas access to raw materials and factory output helped define success in this last era, access to ideas and the ability to create tangible business value from them will define success in the knowledge economy. Smart money believes this is a long-term, irreversible trend." Inc. Magazine

A Few Facts:

- In the United States alone, technology licensing has generated an estimated $45 billion annually, with licensing globally approaching $100 billion annually. For example, a leading company like IBM has returns from its IP portfolio that are estimated at more than $1 billion annually, which accounts for 12 cents of IBM's earning per share.
- According to The Economist, 75% of the value of companies is attributable to their intellectual property.
- Intellectual-property intensive industries contribute $5 trillion per year to the U.S. economy.
- These industries account for about 35% of gross domestic product and 40 million jobs, including 28% of jobs in the U.S.

Successful Thoughts

1. People are worth what they think they are!

2. Daily visualize the date I will become a multimillionaire.

3. Commit all Goals to Action.

4. A positive mental attitude is the nucleus of all successful endeavors.

5. The opinion and advice of Non-Millionaires will drive you to poverty.

6. More money will always serve your future needs better than less.

7. Success only comes to those people who become success conscious.

8. Every Day in Every Way I Get Better and Better, Wiser and Wiser.

9. Pay yourself first-10% savings, 70% expenses, and 20 % debt reduction.

10. Re-invest 100% of profits until Goals is accomplished.

Reference 1 From: Napoleon Hill and CEO W. Clement Stone, *Success Through a Positive Mental Attitude*

Live your dreams by setting goals and doing the work to reach your goals.

Reginald Grant, MS Ed.

Dream Busters

Almost everyone has or had a "Dream Buster" in their life. It can be parents, siblings, friends, children, significant others or even spouses. Yes, even people you love. I say, "Dream Busters" because they say negative things about your dreams, yet so many times they themselves have no dreams or life goals. They put you down at every opportunity and often stress the obstacles you have to overcome on the path to success. They minimize your achievements or contributions and trivialize your steps toward your achieving your goals and dreams. They can be the most challenging obstacles in your path.

What so many people do not understand is, what I call, "The Rule of Flight". Consider this, in order to reach great heights, one must leave the ground, true? One must dare to fail and when they do, they keep getting up and trying it again. Steadily moving toward accomplishing their goals. When you shoot for the stars and you fall short, you have lifted your spirit, your purpose and your mind to new heights. For example, if your shoot for Mars, 1,000,000 million miles from earth, and you only reach the moon, you've still traveled 100,00 miles from where you started.

 Goal setting and dreaming are an ongoing and constantly evolving process; you set a goal, you plan the steps to accomplish that goal, and then implement the steps to reach the goal. You either reach or don't reach the goal in the specified time and way. You re-evaluate, reprioritize and re-set your goal. It' an ongoing and constant process.

Dream Busters never understand the process or are willing to make a commitment to succeeding and failing along the way. So many times, they are afraid of success.   When you reach that goal or achieve some level of success, the Dream Busters won't acknowledge why or accept that you no longer need their validation or voice.

Manage Your Brand: You Can Pimp Me But, You Must Pay me. Simply means know what you are worth and don't be afraid to ask for it. Understanding your value is important and taking a stand is just as important. Do not be under sold, do not be afraid to articulate that to those that want to leverage your brand or do business with you. Under valuing who you are and want you bring to the table is not a winning strategy. I and I alone (with your team if you have one) should determine what you are worth. I never let anyone else determine my value and neither should you.

YOUTH ENTREPRENEURIAL IMPACT PROGRAM ™ Y.E.I.P.

Empowering Youth with the Entrepreneurial Tools of the Future

VOLUME 1

Reginald Grant, MSEd

*YOUR GUIDE TO STARTING YOUR
BUSINESS*

ENTREPRENEUR

THE BASICS OF BUSINESS

REGINALD GRANT

www.ingramcontent.com/pod-product-compliance
Lightning Source LLC
Chambersburg PA
CBHW031504210526
45463CB00003B/1063